DK eyewonder

Pirates

Penguin Random House

LONDON, NEW YORK,
MELBOURNE, MUNICH, and DELHI

Written and edited by Deborah Lock
Designed by Leah Germann
and Tory Gordon-Harris
Publishing manager Susan Leonard
Managing art editor Clare Shedden
Jacket design John Dinsdale
Jacket editor Mariza O'Keefe
Jacket copywriter Adam Powley
Picture researcher Sarah Pownall
Production Luca Bazzoli
DTP designer Almudena Díaz
Consultant Kenneth Kinkor

REVISED EDITION
DK UK
Senior editor Caroline Stamps
Senior art editor Rachael Grady
US editor Margaret Parrish
Jacket editor Manisha Majithia
Jacket designer Nishesh Batnagar, Mark Cavanagh
Jacket design development manager
Sophia M. Tampakopoulos Turner
Producer (print production) Mary Slater
Producer (pre-production) Rachel Ng
Publisher Andrew Macintyre

DK INDIA
Senior editor Shatarupa Chaudhuri
Assistant editor Neha Chaudhary
Art editor Dhirendra Singh
Managing editor Alka Thakur Hazarika
Managing art editor Romi Chakraborty
DTP designer Dheeraj Singh
Picture researcher Sumedha Chopra

First American Edition, 2005
This American Edition, 2015
Published in the United States by DK Publishing
4th floor, 345 Hudson Street
New York, New York 10014
13 14 15 16 17 10 9 8 7 6 5 4 3 2 1
001—196645—02/2015

DK books are available at special discounts when purchased in bulk for
sales promotions, premiums, fund-raising, or educational use. For details,
contact: DK Publishing Special Markets, 345 Hudson Street, New York,
New York 10014 or SpecialSales@dk.com.

Color reproduction by Scanhouse, Malaysia
Printed and bound in China by Hung Hing

Discover more at
www.dk.com

Contents

What is a pirate?

Shiver me timbers! Pirates are sea raiders, attacking other ships and terrorizing coastal towns for booty. But were they really bold adventurers, swashbuckling heroes, or brutal thieves?

The evil pirate Captain Hook—the enemy of Peter Pan

Fictional pirates

There are many stories about pirates and their adventures created in the minds of writers and filmmakers. Even the popular image of what a pirate looks like is mostly made up.

Gold coin from the ship Whydah

TEYE may be the name of the pirate who wore the ring.

Written accounts

There does exist some reliable written evidence of real pirates and what they did. These include pirates' confessions in trial records, logbooks, and even a diary written by a surgeon who sailed on a pirate ship.

Recovered objects

Artifacts such as bottles, tankards, and brass buckles, found in places where pirates came ashore, have provided clues about what they wore and what they did on land.

The promise of riches

Piracy was attractive to many for different reasons: a life offering freedom, lawlessness, and equality. But all pirates were lured by the idea that they could become rich quickly.

Pirates dressed in the fashion of the time.

Expedition *Whydah*

In 1984, the shipwreck of the galley *Whydah* was discovered by underwater explorers. On board, they found treasure, weapons, and personal possessions. The *Whydah* was a pirate ship belonging to Captain Sam Bellamy that sank in 1717.

Bellamy looted treasure from more than 50 ships.

Shipwreck clues

The findings on the wrecks of pirate ships are slightly different from those found on trading or navy ships. These clues help historians to piece together the truth about pirates.

Where were they?

Throughout history, pirates have been sailing in the seas and oceans around the world. Some groups of pirates have been called by different names.

NORTH
AMERICA

Atlantic
Ocean

Caribbean
Sea

SOUTH
AMERICA

Buccaneers

In the 17th century, pirates who raided and stole from treasure ships and settlements around the Caribbean Sea were called buccaneers.

Edward Teach (Blackbeard) was one of the most feared pirates of the Caribbean in the early 18th century.

Pirate words

Freebooter This was another name for a pirate.

Flibustier A French term for a freebooter or plunderer.

Picaroon A word meaning a small-time pirate or slave smuggler, particularly during the 18th century.

Privateers

Some shipowners were given permission by their countries to attack shipping from other countries in wartime. Often they turned to piracy once the war was over.

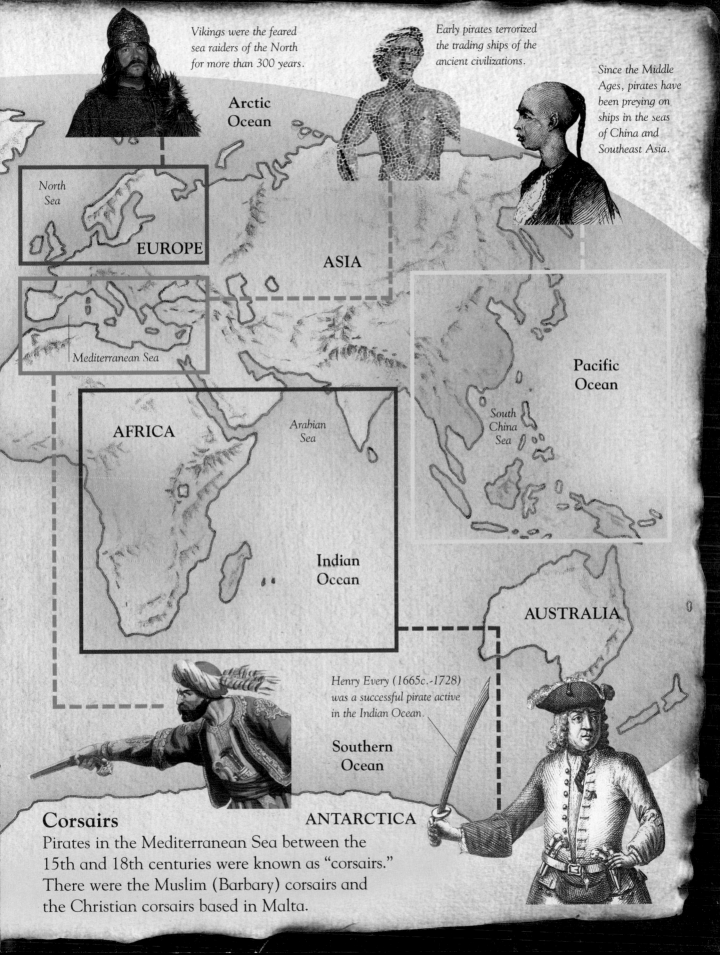

Vikings were the feared sea raiders of the North for more than 300 years.

Early pirates terrorized the trading ships of the ancient civilizations.

Since the Middle Ages, pirates have been preying on ships in the seas of China and Southeast Asia.

Arctic Ocean

North Sea

EUROPE

ASIA

Mediterranean Sea

Pacific Ocean

AFRICA

Arabian Sea

South China Sea

Indian Ocean

AUSTRALIA

Henry Every (1665c.-1728) was a successful pirate active in the Indian Ocean.

Southern Ocean

ANTARCTICA

Corsairs

Pirates in the Mediterranean Sea between the 15th and 18th centuries were known as "corsairs." There were the Muslim (Barbary) corsairs and the Christian corsairs based in Malta.

Early piracy

EUROPE

Mediterranean Sea

Aegean Sea

For more than 2,500 years, pirates have lurked along trading routes, ready to attack loaded merchant ships. The early pirates terrorized those sailing around the Mediterranean Sea.

Pirate myths
Stories about pirates, such as those trying to capture a god hoping to ransom him, were based on people's real fear of being kidnapped by them.

Loaded merchant ships were easy targets as they sailed close to the coastline.

Ready to pounce
The many tiny islands and inlets in the Aegean Sea were superb hiding places for pirates. From here, they could wait and watch for passing merchant ships.

Luring targets

The Phoenician merchant ships carried precious cargo such as silver, tin, copper, and amber, from cities around the Mediterranean Sea. War galleys tried to protect them from the pirates.

These Phoenician coins, called shekels, were made of silver from Spain.

The sharp ram at the front of the pirate galley crashes into the merchant ship.

Trading ships had broad, rounded hulls for storing cargo. They were slow and powered only by sail.

This is an ancient Greek drinking bowl showing a pirate galley attacking a Greek trading ship.

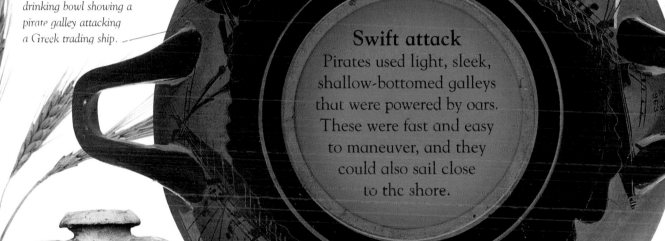

Swift attack
Pirates used light, sleek, shallow-bottomed galleys that were powered by oars. These were fast and easy to maneuver, and they could also sail close to the shore.

Growing menace
Pirates of the Roman world sold their stolen cargoes of wheat, wine, olive oil, and kidnapped slaves at local markets for a good price.

Pirate hunter
In 67 BCE, a large fleet of Roman warships led by Pompey the Great rounded up the pirates. The Roman army also attacked the pirates' base in Cilicia, Turkey.

9

Raiders of the North

Since ancient times, pirates have also been active in the North Sea. The most ferocious raiders were the Vikings from Scandinavia—Norway, Sweden, Finland, and Denmark.

Scandinavia

North Sea

EUROPE

Broad sword

Arrowhead

Helmet

In battle, a Viking trick was to catch a spear in midflight and hurl it back at his opponent.

Homeland and weapons

Life was tough for the people living in the cold regions of Scandinavia. They lived by fishing, farming, and trading, but they wanted adventure, wealth, and glory in battle.

The large rectangular sail picked up the winds on open seas.

Oars were used to row around coasts and up rivers.

Round wooden shield

Sea raiders

The phrase "to go a-viking" means "going on an overseas raid." These fearsome warriors sailed across the North Sea, attacking ships and raiding abbeys and towns in Europe and North America.

The strong keel held the boat together in stormy seas.

The steering oar was attached to the back of the boat.

Vikings made jewelry from stolen gold.

Longship
Vikings were great shipbuilders. They built very long, narrow ships to carry their warriors for the raids.

The sight of approaching longships would cause panic and fear among the villagers or monks.

Plunder
The Vikings were after the valuable items from abbeys, and jewelry, money, and fine cloth from large towns. They either sold these at a good price in other countries or took them home.

A carving of an animal head, such as a snake or dragon

Viking facts

● Some Viking warriors were called berserkers because they attacked so fiercely.

● Viking women were taught to use weapons in case they were attacked.

● Vikings used horns as drinking cups.

EUROPE

Mediterranean Sea

NORTH AFRICA

Barbary corsairs

From the late 11th century, Christians and Muslims fought for control of the Mediterranean Sea and the countries around it. These holy wars were known as the Crusades. The Muslim sea raiders became known as the Barbary corsairs.

Captives' fate

Captured wealthy Christian knights would be held for ransom. The poorer captives were forced to row the Barbary galleys day and night and then sold as slaves.

Muslim galleys

The fast, sleek Barbary ships were powered by huge numbers of slaves. They could only spend a short time at sea, since food and water supplies ran out quickly. The ship's captain, or "rais," navigated the ship.

Each oar was pulled by up to six slaves.

A Barbary galley had one large triangular sail and a slim hull.

Dragut Rais was a feared captain of the Muslim navy.

The brothers

Kheir-ed-Din and Aruj were great Muslim naval heroes in the 1500s. They made their fortunes capturing the Pope's galleys, Spanish warships, and trading ships.

The brothers were known as the "Barbarossa Brothers" in Europe because of their red beards.

Sea battles

After a Barbary galley rammed the side of a Christian ship, about 100 janissaries—well-trained Muslim soldiers—stormed aboard and overpowered the crew.

Many Christian ships were easily overcome by the successful attacks of the Barbary corsairs.

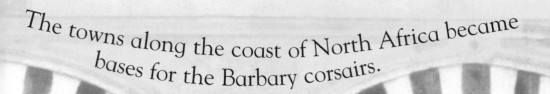

The Maltese revenge

In 1530, Malta—an island in the Mediterranean Sea—became the base for the Christian knights defending the sea routes from Barbary control.

Maltese Cross
The eight-pointed cross worn by the knights represented the eight codes they followed, such as "live in truth," "have faith," "love justice," and "be sincere."

Headstrong knights
The armor of these Maltese corsairs was made from heavy metal. They fought with a rapier in one hand and a dagger for defense in the other.

From the raised forecastle, the corsairs jumped down onto the Barbary galleys.

The triangular sails made the galley easier to maneuver.

Helmets were shaped to deflect blows.

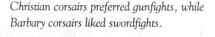
Christian corsairs preferred gunfights, while Barbary corsairs liked swordfights.

Christian galleys
The Maltese corsairs had fast, sleek galleys similar to those of the Muslims, but the boats were powered by two large triangular sails and had fewer oars. The galleys also had more guns.

Round Italian targe (target) shield with simple engraving

Fortresses
When the knights arrived in Malta, they built fortresses, watchtowers, hospitals, and churches. After the Muslims' attack in 1565, Maltese cities and defenses had to be completely rebuilt.

"Turned Turk"

Some European pirates, such as Sir Francis Verney, joined the Barbary corsairs on their raids to Ireland and Iceland.

Strong Maltese forts protected the harbors.

DECISIVE VICTORY

The last great galley battle was fought in 1571 at Lepanto, near Greece. The Maltese knights joined a large Christian fleet powered by 50,000 oarsmen and carrying 30,000 soldiers against the powerful Muslim navy. After a four-hour battle, the Muslim navy was defeated with only 40 of their 300 galleys still afloat.

The New World

From 1492, Spanish ships brought back gold and silver treasures stolen from the local people of the "New World"— the Americas. Other countries and pirates began to notice and were eager to share in the prize.

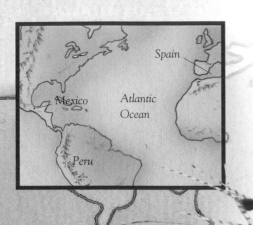

Spain
Atlantic Ocean
Mexico
Peru

Columbus led four voyages to the Caribbean, searching for gold and claiming the land for Spain.

Caribbean Sea

Peru

By the 1500s, the Aztec people controlled much of Mexico, while the Incas from Peru were powerful in South America.

The western trade route
Christopher Columbus sailed across the Atlantic Ocean looking for a route to Asia. He landed in the Bahamas and was given amazing gifts by the local people.

Spanish convoys

● Spanish galleons were loaded with treasure in Mexico or Panama and then met at Havana in Cuba for their return trip to Europe.

● Twice a year, up to 100 treasure ships traveled in a convoy across the Atlantic.

The Incas used gold for decoration and for honoring their gods, but not as money.

The Spanish Main
Further adventurers from Spain sailed west and claimed even more of the American mainland from Mexico to Peru as part of the Spanish empire.

Spanish treasure ships were attacked by pirates during the early stages of their voyages.

Treasure ships

In 1523, the pirate Jean Florin was the first to attack the fully loaded Spanish caravels returning from the Spanish Main. After this, the Spanish organized convoys of larger, well-armed galleons.

Spanish galleons had a crew of 200 men and up to 60 cannons, but were slower than the pirate ships.

Spain

The king and queen of Spain supported Columbus's trips.

Before 1492, maps did not include the Americas. There was only ocean between Africa and Asia.

Columbus' ships were called the Niña, the Pinta, and the Santa María.

Destructive greed

The conquistadors (conquerors) wanted the gold and silver treasures of the Aztecs and the Incas. Their ruthlessness completely destroyed these ancient American civilizations.

The Inca king Atahualpa was ransomed for a room full of gold treasures.

Cortés—friend or foe?

The Spanish conquistador Hernán Cortés was treated like a god by the Aztecs in Mexico. But his Spanish army destroyed their great city, Tenochtitlan.

Aztec treasures were crushed or melted to save space on the Spanish ships.

Privateers

Not all pirates were outlaws. There was one group, called privateers, that was allowed to attack enemy ships. They killed the sailors and stole the treasure to give to their king or queen.

Gold

Saffron

Cinnamon sticks

Turmeric

The Queen's favorite

There were three famous privateers during the reign of Queen Elizabeth I: Thomas Cavendish, John Hawkins, and Sir Francis Drake. The Queen called Drake "my pirate," because he made her very rich.

Friend or foe

Using a telescope, a privateer captain could see the flag of the target ship. He would raise the flag of a friendly nation, so that he could sail close. He would speak through the trumpet to make demands for surrender.

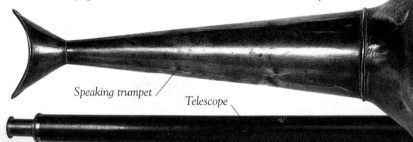

Speaking trumpet

Telescope

PEG LEGS AND PARROTS

If a pirate's leg was badly injured, it would be cut off by the ship's carpenter. Often the pirate would die. If he survived, a piece of wood might replace the leg. The French privateer François le Clerc was nicknamed "Jambe-de-Bois" (Peg leg) because of his wooden leg. As for parrots, it is thought unlikely that pirates kept parrots as pets.

License to kill

Privateers were given royal letters of permission to attack enemy ships during wartime. But some greedy privateers attacked ships from any country and kept the treasure.

It took four days to load all of the treasure from one Spanish galleon onto this ship.

The *Golden Hinde*

In 1580, Drake returned to England on board his small ship, the *Golden Hinde*. He had successfully sailed around the world, attacking ships along the way. His ship was packed full of exotic spices and stolen treasure.

El Draque

Due to his devastating raids on the ports of the Spanish Main, Drake was greatly feared by the Spanish. They referred to him as El Draque ("the Dragon").

Privateer ships were smaller, faster, and easier to maneuver than the Spanish ships.

These ships were crowded with extra crewmen to sail any captured ships.

Drake's ship the Pelican was renamed the Golden Hinde.

Buccaneers

NORTH AMERICA

Caribbean Islands

SOUTH AMERICA

During the 1600s, many outlaws, escaped slaves, and adventurers went to live in the Caribbean. They formed a group of lawless buccaneers who attacked trading ships and raided ports.

Origin of their name

The early buccaneers lived peacefully as pig hunters on the island of Hispaniola. The natives showed them how to build racks, called boucans, for smoking and preserving the meat.

The dried meat and hides were traded to passing ships.

The gold coins were called doubloons.

Pieces of eight

The Spanish turned their silver and gold from the New World into coins, which the buccaneers stole and used as their currency. The silver pieces of eight could be cut into pieces for small change.

Sir Henry Morgan

Between 1663 and 1671, this Welsh captain led large armies of buccaneers on daring, well-planned attacks against Spanish colonies, such as Panama. He was given an English knighthood and made governor of Jamaica.

Bloodthirsty

Some buccaneer captains became infamous for violently torturing and murdering their prisoners. The Frenchman François L'Ollonais, who led the cruelest gang, once cut out the heart of a Spanish prisoner and tore it with his teeth.

Port Royal

The noisy streets of this harbor town in British-controlled Jamaica were filled with swaggering, drunken buccaneers spending their booty. After Morgan's death, it became the place where pirates were tried and hanged. An earthquake destroyed the town in 1692.

Brethren of the coast

In 1630, the Spanish attacked the settlers on Hispaniola. Many of them escaped and became pirates, raiding Spanish treasure ships. The pirates governed themselves, and booty from the raids was shared fairly.

The Jolly Roger

Ships have always flown flags. Some show which country the ship belongs to; others might show where the ship is headed. But the skull and crossbones of the Jolly Roger meant only one thing—pirates!

A sign from the grave

About 400 years ago, the skull-and-crossbones symbol was used by ordinary people as a sign of death. The pirates took this and other symbols from gravestones and turned them into threatening flags that would scare other ships' crews.

Around 1700, the skull-and-crossbones symbol first appeared on a pirate's flag.

Surrender, or else

The black-and-white Jolly Roger flag was raised as a warning to surrender without a fight. If the captain of the target ship refused to stop, the pirates would raise a red flag to signal an attack. This would mean a fight to the death.

Changing faces

Every pirate captain had his own flag design, and not all pirates used the same symbols. This skull sits on top of crossed swords instead of bones. It belonged to the Caribbean pirate Jack Rackham.

Red for danger

Not all pirates' flags were black—the most fearsome had red flags, which meant that the pirates would show no mercy. It is thought that the flag got the name "Jolly Roger" from the French words *jolie rouge*, meaning "pretty red."

Swords and daggers were shown as symbols of power and a willingness to kill.

Death was also called Old Roger— another reason why the flag was called a Jolly Roger.

Old Roger was also a nickname for the Devil.

A toast to death

Bartholomew Roberts was a very successful pirate who sank more than 400 ships off the African and Caribbean coasts. His flag showed him drinking with Death.

Needle and thread

The pirate ship's flag was roughly made. It was either painted, or it was sewn by the ship's sailmaker or any crew member who could use a needle.

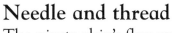

Still flying high

Beware—the Jolly Roger is still in use today! It is flown on British Royal Navy submarines returning to port—a tradition started during World War I. The flag was made by the crew of the submarine, celebrating a successful return home. It showed events that happened during their time at sea, such as how many enemy ships were sunk.

The Pirate Round

During the 17th century, European countries began to send large merchant ships to trade with India and China. Many pirates followed them to the Indian Ocean to seek their fortunes.

The Round

Lured by the riches that could be taken from the Indian treasure fleets and European trade ships, pirates from North America sailed thousands of miles to the Indian Ocean and back again with their booty.

NORTH AMERICA

The route of the Pirate Round

Atlantic Ocean

Caribbean Sea

SOUTH AMERICA

The wild, tropical island of Madagascar was a safe place for outlaws to rest.

Pirates' lair

The pirates found an ideal base on the island of Madagascar. There were few people, no laws, and no fresh food and water supplies, and the trading ships passed close by.

Repairing

Pirates needed safe beaches to remove the seaweed and barnacles from the bottoms of their ships and repair any holes. This was called careening.

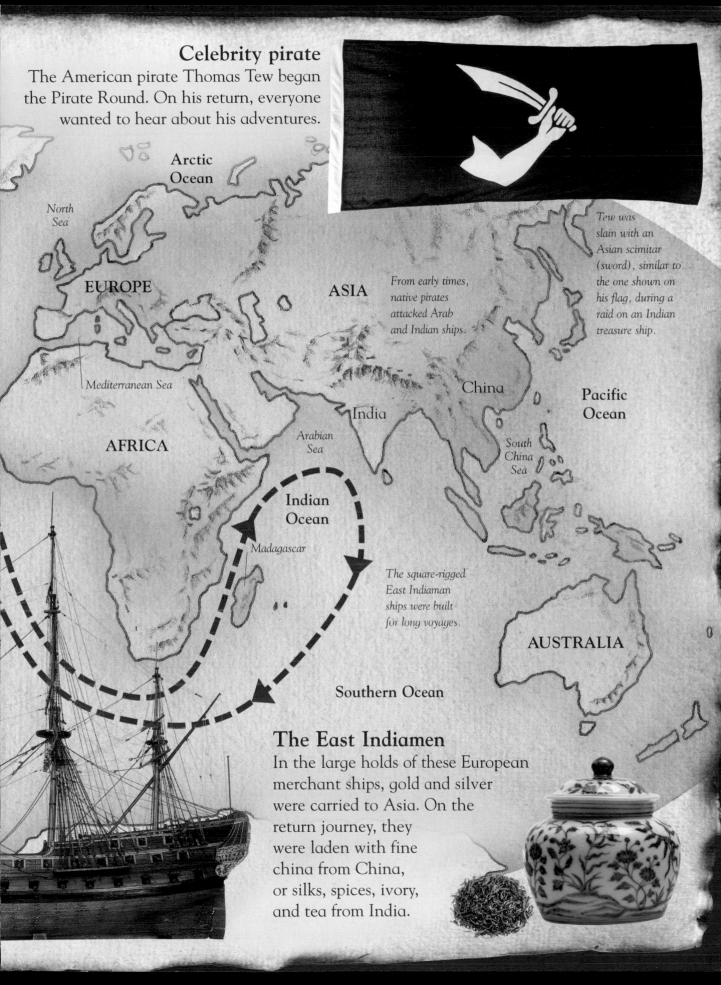

Celebrity pirate

The American pirate Thomas Tew began the Pirate Round. On his return, everyone wanted to hear about his adventures.

Arctic
Ocean

North
Sea

EUROPE

Mediterranean Sea

AFRICA

ASIA

From early times, native pirates attacked Arab and Indian ships.

China

India

Arabian
Sea

Pacific
Ocean

South
China
Sea

Tew was slain with an Asian scimitar (sword), similar to the one shown on his flag, during a raid on an Indian treasure ship.

Indian
Ocean

Madagascar

The square-rigged East Indiaman ships were built for long voyages.

AUSTRALIA

Southern Ocean

The East Indiamen

In the large holds of these European merchant ships, gold and silver were carried to Asia. On the return journey, they were laden with fine china from China, or silks, spices, ivory, and tea from India.

Attack!

If a ship's captain refused to surrender to the pursuing pirates, then attack was likely. Cannon fire from the pirates' ship signaled the start of the fight.

Boom!

Upon hitting the wooden sides, a flying cannonball would send a deadly spray of wooden splinters onto the decks. Cannon fire was used to slow down the enemy ship.

This 18th-century cannon is balanced on a circular pivot. Its aim can be raised or lowered by moving the wedge at the back.

Two cannonballs chained together could bring down masts and sails.

A pirate marksman needed calm seas to aim his musket carefully.

A musket ball was wrapped in a patch of cloth.

Patches were kept in patchboxes.

Hand-to-hand

Amid a cloud of gunsmoke, pirates climbed aboard the enemy ship, yelling and threatening. Ruthless and determined, they were well armed for the fierce hand-to-hand fighting that followed.

Aim, fire!

Before boarding, a marksman would aim his long musket to kill the steerer of the ship. Upon boarding, a pirate fired his pistol and then used the hard butt as a club. A musketoon was used when he got close to his victims.

The musketoon was fired from the shoulder.

Sea air sometimes dampened the powder in a pistol, and the gun would misfire with a quiet "flash in the pan."

Pistols were light and easy to carry, but were slow to reload.

Pirates only had time to fire once from their cannons before boarding.

Cutthroat cutlass

The short, broad blade of a cutlass was the perfect weapon for fighting on a ship. A longer blade would get tangled in a ship's rigging.

The spikes of these caltrops, or crowsfeet, thrown on deck could cause terrible injuries.

Ax attack

When attacking a large vessel, pirates used their axes to help climb the ship's wooden sides. Once on deck, the axes were used to cut through the ropes holding up the sails.

Ramrod for pushing the ball and patch into the barrel

Dangerous daggers

Pirates often had daggers tucked away under their clothes for a surprise attack. These small, deadly weapons were also ideal for use on the lower decks, where there was no space to swing a sword.

The sharp blade of an ax could cut through a rope as thick as a man's arm.

A dagger was kept in a sheath.

PIRATE WOMEN

Women were not allowed on board pirate ships. However, some wanted the freedom and adventure. Dressed in pirate's clothing, they acted like men and often fought more fiercely than many men. Mary Read and Anne Bonny joined the pirate crew of Jack Rackham. They were a fearsome duo, and were the only members of the crew brave enough to fight when their ship was captured in 1720.

Scuttled!

In the 1630s, the pirate David Jones sank a ship he had captured because it was no longer seaworthy. Since then, the term "Davy Jones's locker" refers to anything that has been sent to the sea floor on purpose.

A pirate's life for me

A pirate attack was exciting and dangerous, but during the weeks at sea in between these raids, pirates could become bored and irritable on the crowded ships.

Shipshape

Many crew members were kept busy with the constant need for altering the sails and rigging to keep the ship moving. Other jobs included mending any broken ropes and sails and cleaning their weapons.

Pirates ate tough, dried biscuits called "hard tack" in the dark to keep from seeing the weevils crawling on them.

There was little variety or nutrition in the diet of the pirates.

Food and drink

Hens were often kept on board to provide fresh eggs and meat. Fish were also caught. In the Caribbean, turtles were caught and stored on board. Fresh water quickly became undrinkable, so food was washed down with beer or wine.

Ship words

Bilge The lowest part of a ship that fills with slimy water.

Block and tackle The pulleys and ropes of the rigging supporting the masts and sails.

Crow's nest A lookout platform near the top of the mast.

Life below decks

As for any seaman, life on board a pirate ship was cramped, damp, and filthy. Below decks, there was the smell of rotting water, tar, and unwashed bodies. In the dark, pirates dreamed about life on land.

Pieces of eight

Dice

Cards

The Execution of the mur therers of S.E.B Godfree

Yo ho ho...

On many pirate ships, gambling for money was not allowed, to prevent fights on board. However, on reaching a port, pirates could spend their booty on having a wild time.

A large barrel was known as a hogshead.

Rats were a nuisance and often ate the food supplies.

... and a bottle of rum

Innkeepers welcomed the thirsty pirates into their dockside taverns. Tankards made from pewter or leather were filled and refilled with beer, wine, or even rum. Pirates were often drunk on shore.

Marooned

Some pirate crews voted and agreed to obey a code of conduct while on board. However, if a pirate broke the rules, such as stealing from another or deserting the ship during a battle, then as a punishment he would be left behind on a desert island.

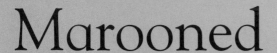

Castaway

A pirate left or stranded on a desert island faced loneliness and little hope of escape or rescue. If the island had no fresh water, food, or shelter, the pirate would die slowly and painfully.

A pistol was useful for warning off wild beasts.

A marooned pirate could only watch helplessly as his pirate ship sailed away.

Code of conduct

Typical pirate rules:

● Everyone has a vote on all important decisions.

● Everyone has an equal share of the fresh food and drink.

● Lights and candles to be put out at eight o'clock at night.

Short supplies

A disgraced pirate would be marooned with only the clothes he wore, a small bottle of water, a pistol or a musket, and a small amount of shot and gunpowder. He would have to find food and drink if he was to survive.

Musket balls

Gunpowder

A bottle filled with one day's supply of water

PIRATE PUNISHMENTS

Some of the worst punishments given to pirates who broke the rules, or to prisoners, included "kissing the gunner's daughter"— bending over one of the ship's guns and being flogged—and execution by shooting or hanging. Stories about prisoners "walking the plank"—being forced off the end of a board into the sea—have been made up.

The real "Crusoe"

The fictional character Robinson Crusoe was based on the true story of Alexander Selkirk. For five years, Selkirk survived on an island before being rescued. He even taught wild cats and goats to dance.

Shipwreck

Pirates could also find themselves stranded if their leaky ship ran aground, or if they were too drunk to navigate and their ship crashed into rocks. A passing ship was their only hope of rescue.

Edward England was an English pirate captain.

Too kind

England's crew voted to maroon their captain because he was treating a prisoner too well. Along with two other crew members, England was left on the island of Mauritius. They built a boat and escaped to Madagascar.

33

Pirates of the Indian Ocean

Some pirates who sailed to the Indian Ocean to attack shipping were very successful. The stories of the treasure they captured and the fortunes they made have become legendary.

The Red Fort in Delhi, India, was a palace for the Mogul emperors, such as Aurangzeb.

The Great Mogul
The emperor of northern India, Aurangzeb was a religious man and very wealthy. Once a year, a fleet of his ships carrying pilgrims and treasure sailed between Surat in India and Mecca. The ships were a magnet for pirates.

The "Arch-Pirate"
The pirate captain Henry Every became famous for seizing the largest load of treasure after his brutal capture of the Mogul's ship *Gang-i-Sawai* returning from Mecca.

The prize

The precious gems stolen from Indian ships were not always easy to divide equally among the pirate crews, who were each given one share. The captain received a double share.

Sparkling jewelry

Fine silk material

Large quantities of gems, such as rubies

Captain Every's flag

Flying from Every's ship, the *Fancy* was a flag showing a variation on the skull-and-crossbones design. The bandanna and earring have become popular symbols of pirate costumes.

Every facts

● Henry Every was also known as John Avery and Benjamin Bridgeman.

● In 1694, he led a mutiny and took over a privateer's ship and became a pirate captain.

● It is believed that he lost all his wealth and died a poor man.

Unlucky pirate

The Great Mogul was furious about Henry Every's brutal attack on his fleet. He threatened to stop trading with the British government unless they acted to stop the pirates.

Respectable

Scottish-born William Kidd was a well-respected sea captain and shipowner in New York. In 1695, he was given a royal commission by the British king to hunt down the pirates in the Indian Ocean.

In pirate folklore, it is said that a dead man was left to protect the loot.

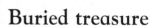

Turned traitor

Rather than tracking down the pirates, Kidd and the crew of the *Adventure Galley* attacked merchant ships, including the huge *Quedagh Merchant*, and took the booty.

Many mysteries surround the sites of Kidd's buried gold.

Buried treasure

Kidd buried much of his treasure so that he did not have to admit how much he had stolen. One of the spots was on Gardiner Island, near New York, but this hoard was found.

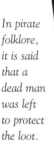

The gates of Newgate Prison in London, where Kidd was held for more than a year before his trial

Kidd's trial took place at the Old Bailey, London, in May 1701.

Kidd's ships

● The *Adventure Galley* had 34 cannons and 150 crew.

● After capturing the huge treasure ship *Quedagh Merchant*, Kidd used the ship to sail back to the Caribbean.

● Kidd renamed the ship the *Adventure Prize*.

Accused

At his trial, Kidd said his crew had forced him to loot the merchant ships. The crew members there denied this, and Kidd was sentenced to hang as a pirate.

Captured

Kidd's actions and failure angered the Mogul emperor further. On his return to New York, Kidd was arrested and sent to prison in England.

Hanged

In 1701, Kidd was hanged at London's Execution Dock. The first rope snapped, so he was hanged on the second attempt. His body was left to hang in chains along the Thames River for years.

It's likely that pirates' maps, where "X" marks the spot of buried treasure, are just a myth.

Punishment

From early times, pirates faced execution if they were caught and convicted. Privateers were imprisoned in dreadful conditions, with little hope of ever being released.

Gallows words

Jack Ketch A pirate's nickname for the hangman.

Hempen halter The noose that was placed around the pirate's neck at the gallows.

Dance the hempen jig To hang from the end of the hangman's hemp rope.

Life in a cell

Pirates were held in prisons before their trials. These were overcrowded, damp, and very unhealthy places. Prisoners had to pay for candles and food. Richer ones bribed the jailers for better cells.

Gallows

Most pirates were executed by hanging. Large crowds would gather to watch the event. Pirates' last words were often written down.

Usually, new wooden gallows would be built for each execution.

Before his hanging, a prisoner was measured for his gibbet cage.

Under lock and key

While in prison or being shipped to a prison, pirates were held in very heavy metal chains around their wrists and ankles to prevent them from escaping.

Handcuffs and key

Gibbet cage

The bodies of pirates who had been hanged were often put on display as a warning to other seamen. A tight-fitting cage called a gibbet was made to hold the bones in place once the skin had rotted. Some bodies were coated in tar to make them last longer.

Floating jails

To make room for more criminals, old ships were turned into floating prisons. Prisoners were held in the damp, stinking holds and fed rotten meat, moldy bread, and stale water. Captured French privateers dreaded the English prison hulks, which they called pontons.

The laundry was hung out to dry.

A blacksmith made the iron cage.

Soldiers guarded the prison hulks.

Tiny windows allowed little fresh air in or unhealthy air out.

The king of pirates

NORTH AMERICA
South Carolina
Bahamas

At the beginning of the 18th century, the Bahamas became the base for a new generation of pirates in the Caribbean. The most terrifying pirate leader at this time was known as Blackbeard.

From this watchtower, the Danes looked out for enemy ships entering the harbor.

Blackbeard's castle

The Skytsbord Tower, built by the Danes in 1679 on the highest point of St. Thomas, one of the US Virgin Islands, has become known as Blackbeard's castle. It is said that he used the tower to look out for trading ships to attack.

Blackbeard facts

● He was an Englishman named Edward Teach (or Drummond, Thatch, or Tash).

● There are many stories about his evil acts of cruelty.

● His rule of terror as a pirate captain lasted only two years, but he had become a legend.

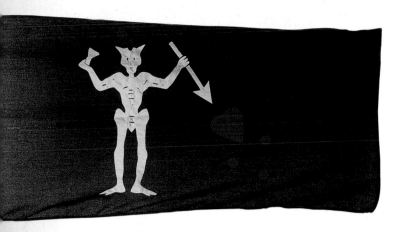

The devil with an hourglass

From his ship, the *Queen Anne's Revenge*, Blackbeard flew his flag, which meant time was running out for his victims. At the sight of this flag, many of the ships he approached surrendered quickly.

The hemp cord was soaked in a liquid that smoldered when lit.

Scary

Before he went into battle, Blackbeard wove hemp cord into his hair and set this alight, placing the smoldering fuses under his hat. He appeared in a thick black cloud of smoke to scare his victims.

Blackbeard carried six pistols, two swords, and a number of knives. Even his crew feared him.

Medicine raids

In 1718, Blackbeard blockaded the harbor of Charleston, South Carolina. He ransomed a member of the town's council and a child in exchange for a chest of medicines.

The doctor's chest was always taken from a captured ship.

Pirates had to steal everyday items, such as food and medicines.

Blackbeard's head was hung on the front of Maynard's ship, HMS Pearl.

The end of an era

In 1718, Blackbeard was finally hunted down in the Ocracoke inlet, North Carolina, by the British navy. He was killed in a famous duel with Lieutenant Maynard.

Pirates of the Eastern Seas

ASIA
Japan
China
South China Sea
Strait of Malacca

For over 1,600 years, ruthless pirates have threatened shipping and coastal towns in eastern Asia. They ranged from small tribal groups in light, speedy boats hiding among the mangrove swamps to large, well-armed fleets roaming the coastline.

Older junks had sails made from bamboo matting.

Junks usually have three masts with four sideways sails.

Pirate junks

Armed with 10 to 15 guns, cargo junks were altered to become feared Chinese pirate fighting ships. From the 17th century, powerful pirates had large fleets of junks, and the Chinese and Japanese navy were unable to defeat them.

Colorful flags

The large pirate fleets were split into groups that each had their own colored flag. The pirates worshiped the goddess T'en Hou, who sometimes appeared on their flags.

天后聖母

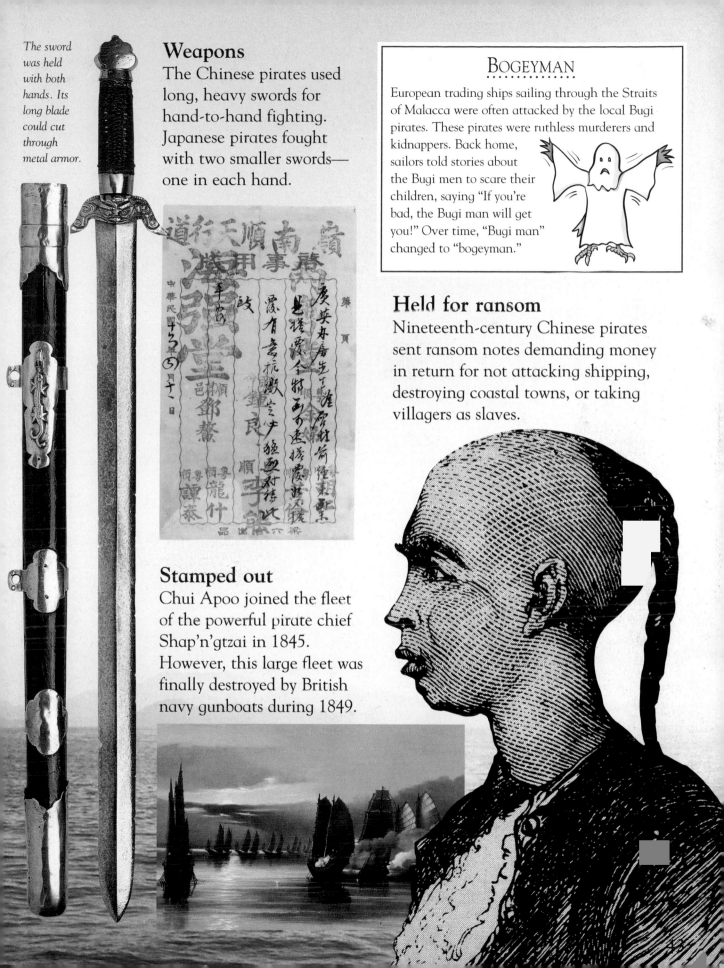

The sword was held with both hands. Its long blade could cut through metal armor.

Weapons

The Chinese pirates used long, heavy swords for hand-to-hand fighting. Japanese pirates fought with two smaller swords—one in each hand.

Held for ransom

Nineteenth-century Chinese pirates sent ransom notes demanding money in return for not attacking shipping, destroying coastal towns, or taking villagers as slaves.

Stamped out

Chui Apoo joined the fleet of the powerful pirate chief Shap'n'gtzai in 1845. However, this large fleet was finally destroyed by British navy gunboats during 1849.

Pirates of today

The threat of an attack by pirates continues today. Some gangs of modern-day pirates use the most up-to-date weapons and technology for their daring raids.

High speed
When ships have to slow down to pass through narrow channels between islands, they are most at risk from a surprise attack from pirates, approaching in high-speed motorboats or dinghies.

Many pirates are heavily armed with machine guns, knives, and mortars.

Pirates climb aboard using grappling hooks and ropes, or poles.

Modern piracy

● In 2012, 297 pirate attacks were reported around the world.

● Most attacks occurred in the waters of east and west Africa.

● Most ships are attacked while at anchor.

● There were 28 ships hijacked in 2012.

Technology

Some well-organized gangs use radio, radar, and global positioning systems (GPS) to track the ship they have chosen to attack. They steal cargo worth millions of dollars while the ship's crew sleeps.

A global positioning system uses satellites to help people navigate.

The Piracy Reporting Center provides information and investigates pirate attacks around the world.

Aircraft and helicopters watch shipping lanes.

Fighting pirates

Well-equipped special forces and coast guards are trained to patrol the seas and investigate pirate attacks. Ships are encouraged to stay alert and in constant contact by radio.

Training exercises recreate a real raid.

Hijacked

Some pirates take over a ship and create a "phantom ship." They repaint and rename the vessel, make false papers, and then offer to carry a cargo. However, they sail to a different port to sell the cargo themselves.

The cash for port charges and paying the crew would be kept inside a ship's safe.

Safe-breakers

The most common pirate raids are those on merchant ships or luxury yachts. The pirates act quickly to take any money or possessions from those on board and then escape.

Set sail

Set sail and see if you can navigate your pirate ship past various obstacles to be the first to find a safe base, or lair. Good luck!

Strong current!
Move forward 3

Hijacked!
Roll a 6 to continue

Stop to look for treasure.
Skip a turn

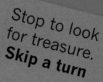

Change route to steer clear of coral.
Move back 4

Strong winds!
Move forward 6

START

Change course to avoid other pirates.
Move back 1

FINISH

You are the first to find a safe base!

Capture a faster ship.
Move forward 4

Speed up to get away from another ship.
Move forward 5

Ship struck by cannon fire.
Move back 5

Compass stops working.
Move back 4

Stop for supplies.
Skip a turn

Find a treasure map in a bottle.
Roll again

True or false?

A lot of what we think we know about pirates is based on what has been seen in movies and read about in stories. See if you can spot the ones that are true.

Certain pirates were sometimes employed by **kings and queens.**
See page 18

Pirates kept **parrots** as pets, placing them on their shoulders.
See page 18

A **disgraced pirate** might have found himself left on an isolated island.
See page 32

The Jolly Roger flag was based on an original image of a laughing man. See page 22

Sometimes pirates buried their **stolen goods** in treasure chests, usually on deserted islands.
See page 36

Edward Teach (Blackbeard) would appear with strands of burning cords in his hair.
See pages 40-41

Pirates drew **treasure maps** with "X" marking the buried treasure.
See page 37

Pirate flags were always **black**. See page 23

There are many imaginary stories about pirates making captured sailors **walk the plank.**
See page 33

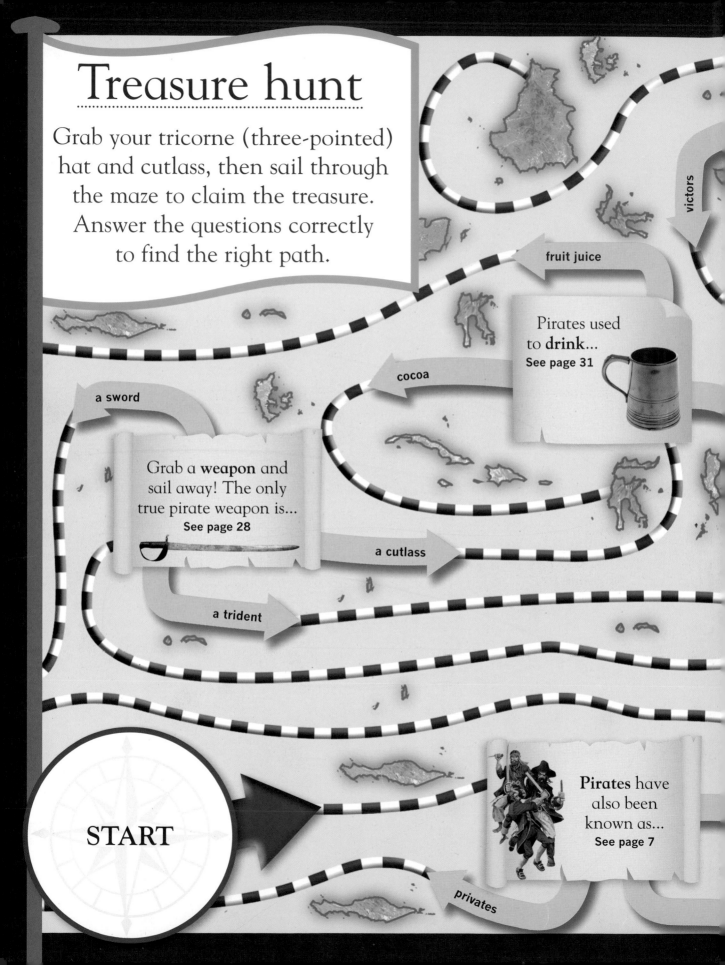

Treasure hunt

Grab your tricorne (three-pointed) hat and cutlass, then sail through the maze to claim the treasure. Answer the questions correctly to find the right path.

victors

fruit juice

Pirates used to drink...
See page 31

cocoa

a sword

Grab a **weapon** and sail away! The only true pirate weapon is...
See page 28

a cutlass

a trident

START

Pirates have also been known as...
See page 7

privates

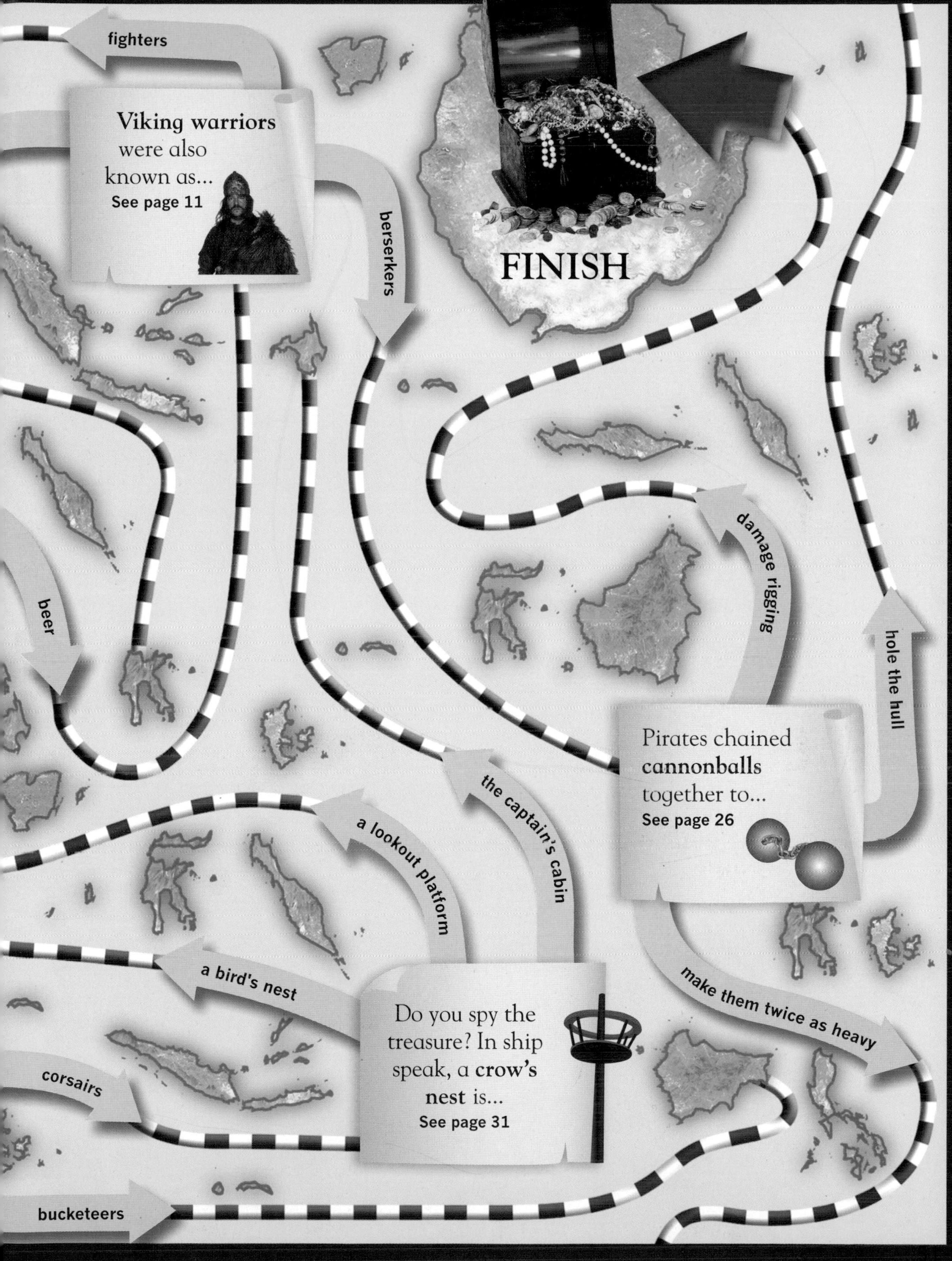

fighters

Viking warriors were also known as...
See page 11

berserkers

FINISH

beer

damage rigging

hole the hull

the captain's cabin

a lookout platform

Pirates chained **cannonballs** together to...
See page 26

a bird's nest

Do you spy the treasure? In ship speak, a **crow's nest** is...
See page 31

make them twice as heavy

corsairs

bucketeers

Facts matchup

How much do you know about pirates? Read the clues and see if you can match them with the correct images.

Before boarding an enemy ship, a marksman would use this to kill the ship's steerer. See page 28

Vikings built these to carry their warriors for raids. See page 11

A privateer captain used this to see the flag of the target ship. See page 18

This was raised to identify a ship's crew as pirates. See page 22

Pirates ate these in the dark to keep from seeing the weevils on them. See page 30

Pirates sold this, among other things, at local markets. See page 9

Pirates kept this on board the ship to provide fresh eggs and meat. See page 30

Jewelry

Pistol

Maltese Cross

Helmet

Cannonballs

Blackbeard

Telescope

Hen

Longship

Blackbeard's flag

Olive oil

Dagger

Jolly Roger flag

Musket

Handcuffs

Gallows

Viking

Hard tack

Rat

If a pirate was captured, these were locked around his wrists to prevent escape. **See page 39**

Large crowds gathered to watch a pirate being hanged from this. **See page 38**

Two of these chained and fired together could bring down masts and sails. **See page 26**

These ferocious warriors from Scandinavia attacked ships and raided abbeys and towns in Europe and North America. **See page 10**

This was flown aboard the ship *Queen Anne's Revenge*. **See page 41**

This piece of armor was worn by a Maltese corsair. **See page 14**

This weapon was light and easy to carry, but slow to reload. **See page 28**

A troublemaker, this creature ate food supplies on the ship. **See page 31**

Vikings stole items such as this from abbeys. **See page 11**

He carried six pistols and appeared in a thick black cloud of smoke to scare his victims. **See page 41**

This was kept in a sheath and pirates tucked it away under their clothes for a surprise attack. **See page 29**

This represented the eight codes of a band of Maltese knights who protected the Mediterranean Sea from pirates. **See page 14**

Glossary

Here are the meanings of some words that are useful to know when you are learning about pirates.

Artifact an object from the past that provides clues about how people lived.

Bandanna a large colorful handkerchief sometimes tied around the head.

Barnacle a small sea creature that clings to rocks and the bottom of ships.

Blockade to stop ships or supplies from entering a port.

Booty goods that are stolen or taken through violence.

Buccaneer a pirate attacking ships in the Caribbean in the 17th century.

Callipers used for measuring on sea charts

Caravel a small ship with three sails used by the Spanish and Portuguese in the 15th and early 16th centuries.

Careen to clean and repair a ship on a beach.

Cargo goods carried on a ship.

Commission permission given to a privateer to attack enemy shipping.

Convoy a group of ships sailing together, protected by the navy.

Corsair a pirate active in the Mediterranean Sea between the 15th and 18th centuries.

Cutlass a short sword used by sailors.

Doubloon a Spanish gold coin.

East Indiaman a large sailing ship used for trading between Europe and Asia in the 17th and 18th centuries.

Execution the punishment of being put to death as a criminal.

Galleon a large ship with square sails used by the Spanish in the 16th and 17th centuries.

Galley a ship powered by oars and sails used in the Mediterranean Sea; a ship's kitchen.

Gallows a post-and-beam-structure used for hanging criminals.

Gambling playing a game for money or possessions.

Gibbet an iron frame for displaying criminals who have been hanged.

Gunboat a warship powered by sails and steam, used in the 19th century.

Compass

Hard tack a stale ship's biscuit.

Hijack to take over control of a ship or its cargo by force.

Hold (of a ship) a place for storing goods.

Hull the main frame of a ship.

Infamous well-known for doing bad deeds.

Jolly Roger a pirate's flag.

Junk a ship with sideways sails used in East Asia.

Keel a piece of wood along the center of the bottom of a ship.

Kidnap to take a person by force.

Letters of marque official papers given to privateers.

Longship a Viking's sailing ship.

Maneuver to change the position of a ship.

Maroon to leave someone on a desert island.

Merchant a person who buys and sells goods.

Musket a long-barreled gun.

Navigate to plan and guide the course of a ship with the help of charts and equipment.

Outlaw a person running away from the law.

Pieces of eight a Spanish silver coin that pirates divided into pieces.

Pistol a light, short-barreled gun.

A navigational instrument for telling time

Plunder to take goods by force; booty.

Privateer a shipowner who is given permission by his country to attack and loot other countries' ships.

Raid a surprise attack to steal goods from a place or a person.

Rais a sea captain of the Barbary corsairs.

Ransom to demand money for the release of a captured person.

Rapier a long, straight sword with a narrow pointed blade.

Rigging the ropes and chains used on a ship to support the masts and sails.

Scuttle to sink a ship on purpose.

Share a part of the loot.

Spices plants that are used to flavor and preserve food.

Surrender to hand over control and possessions to someone else after fighting them.

Tar a thick, dark, sticky substance used to seal and preserve objects against the weather.

Tavern an inn or a place that sells drinks.

Viking a Scandinavian warrior and sea trader of the 8th to 10th centuries.

Pirate navigators used simple instruments.

Index

Acknowledgments

Dorling Kindersley would like to thank:
Sarah Mills for picture library services.

Picture credits

The publisher would like to thank the following for their kind permission to reproduce their photographs:
(Key: a-above; c-center; b-below; l-left; r-right; t-top)

akg-images: 16cra, 16cl, 17car. **Alamy Images:** Paul Gapper 12-13; Hemera Technologies 45br; Trevor Smithers ARPS 30tr. **The Art Archive:** 9br, 37br, 43bl; Dagli Orti (A) 14tc; Private Collection /Eileen Tweedy 36tl. **Corbis:** Blue Lantern Studio 36cr; Bob Krist 6br; Bruce Adams; Eye Ubiquitous 40; Danny Lehman 21tl; Fukuhara, Inc. 3; Historical Picture Archive 17clb; Jim Erickson 16crb; Joel W. Rogers 1, 19; Lindsay Hebberd 34-35cra; Nik Wheeler 42; Reuters 17tl, 45c, 56c; Richard T. Nowitz 4cl, 5tl, 30l, 54-55; Sergio Pitamitz 32; Sygma 26-27; Sygma/ Cailleux Sebastien 24cl; Ted Spiegel 11; Wolfgang Kaehler 33br. **Dorling Kindersley:** © Judith Miller /DK /Freeman's 31br; © St Mungo, Glasgow Museums 12cra; British Museum, London 2tcl, 9tl, 9tr, 9bl, 9tc, 9c, 10tr, 11tcl, 17bcl, 17bcr, 18cal, 20bl, 25br, 31tl; Courtesy of the Board of Trustees of the Royal Armouries 28br; Courtesy of the Musee de Saint-Malo, France 18cb, 18cl, 26bl, 39r; National

Maritime Museum, London 10crb, 10bl, 12bc, 14cr, 18tl, 24-25b, 26bc, 28ca, 28cal, 28c, 28crb, 28bl, 28-29t, 28-29cb, 29clb, 29ca, 30crb, 32-33c, 33cla, 38cr, 41cra, 42bl, 43c, 43l; Danish National Museum 10cra, 11tl, 11tc; Michel Zebe 17br; Museum of London 30crb, 31ca, 35r; Museum of the Order of St John, London 14bc, 14bcl, 14bl, 14cbl; Rye Town Council 38-39b, 39tl; Armé Museum, Stockholm, Sweden 52cr, City of London Police 53clb, Danish National Museum 52tr, David Edge's Private Collection 52crb, Ermine Street Guard 53cla, National Maritime Museum, The National Maritime Museum, London 52-53bc, 53cb, Rough Guides 52cra, The Royal Green Jackets Museum, Winchester 52crb (telescope), The Science Museum, London 47cb, The Wallace Collection, London 52tr (pistol). **Dreamstime.com:** Ella Batalon 47tl, Petar Milevski 53clb (Medieval gallows), Onizuka 48cr. **Empics Ltd:** EPA European Press Agency 45tc. **Mary Evans Picture Library:** 6cl, 7bl, 12br, 20r, 21tr, 22cl, 37c. **Kevin Fleming Design and Photography:** 8. **Fotolia:** Alperium 46bl, 49b, Yong Hian Lim 48bl. **Getty Images:** David Hiser 5; JIMIN LAI/AFP 44b; Steve Liss/Time Life Pictures 4bl, 4bc. **Tory Gordon-Harris:** 16bc. **Sonia Halliday Photographs:** 7tc, 8cr. **Lonely Planet Images:** Eoin Clarke 15. **Museum Of London:** 37tl, 38tr. © **National Maritime Museum, London:** 4-5c, 7tr, 13b, 18br, 21b, 24bc, 43br. **Peter Newark's Military Pictures:** 6cb, 19tl, 41bl, 41br. **Richard Platt:** 22tl. **Powerstock:** Ross Armstrong 29. **Rex Features:** Everett Collection 4tl. **Shutterstock:** 48tr. **Topfoto.co.uk:** 2l; 2004 Fotomas 13cl; The British Library /HIP 34tr. **Zefa Visual Media:** Masterfile/Randy Miller 44ca.

All other images © Dorling Kindersley
For further information see: www.dkimages.com